Primary School English Dictionary Key Concepts

First published in 2019 by Succeedu Education Ltd

Copyright © 2019 by Steven Rhodes

All rights reserved. No part of this publication may be reproduced, distributed, or transmitted in any form or by any means, including photocopying, recording, or other electronic or mechanical methods, without the prior written permission of the publisher.

ISBN: 978-1-9160220-1-0

 is a registered trademark of Succeedu Education Ltd.

Succeedu Education Ltd
Kemp House
160 City Road
London
EC1V 2NX
United Kingdom
0203 34880846
info@succeedu.co.uk

www.succeedu-books.com
www.succeedu.co.uk

Cover design
Zest Creative Co., ltd
www.zest-creative.com

For my parents Glenda and Wilman.
Thank you for your love and support.

Introduction

The Primary English dictionary by Succeedu Education uses simple language and illustrations to define the key concepts in the subject.

This dictionary is designed for children, parents and teachers to use a reference so that everybody involved in the learning process is reading from the same page. Supporting young children in developing the ability to independently think, act and search for understanding is a key skill in our rapidly changing world.

This book is written for:

Children: Definitions are simple and easy-to-understand. The pictures and illustrations help young learners consolidate and deepen their learning from the classroom.

Parents: Helping with homework can be a challenge at times and not knowing the current language or processes used in today's primary schools can be frustrating. Use the dictionary as a tool to keep up-to-date with your child's learning.

Teachers: Use the dictionary as a reference for lesson planning or to refresh your understanding.

I hope you find this book useful

Steven

A-Z English Dictionary

abbreviation: A shortened form of a word or phrase. It contains a group of letters taken from the word or phrase.

e.g. = for example

St = street

abstract noun: A noun that refers to a feeling or something that cannot be physically touched .

Idea: Knowledge

Feeling: Happiness

acronym: An abbreviation made from the first letter of each word in a phrase.

NASA = National Aeronautics Space Administration

A-Z English Dictionary

acrostic: A type of poem where the first letter of each line read from top to bottom makes a word.

S oftly falling on the ground.
N ot one flake is ever the same.
O utside laughter and playing sounds.
W inter time is here again.

active voice: Describes a sentence where the subject of the sentence performs the action of the verb. (See passive voice.)

Active voice

Subject	Verb	Object
carries out the action	the action	the action is being done to

The cat chased the mouse.

Passive voice

Object	Verb	Subject
the action is being done to	the action	carries out the action

The mouse was chased by the cat.

adjective: A word that describes a noun or a pronoun.

colourful bird   ramshackle house

A-Z English Dictionary

adjective phrase: A group of words that describe a noun or pronoun.

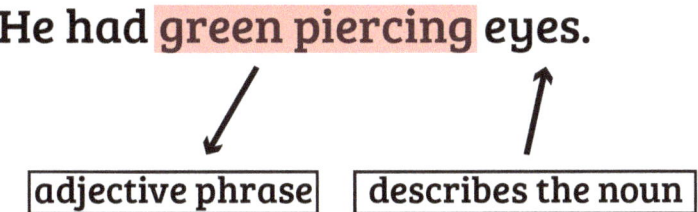

adverb: A single word that gives extra information about the verb (describes the verb).

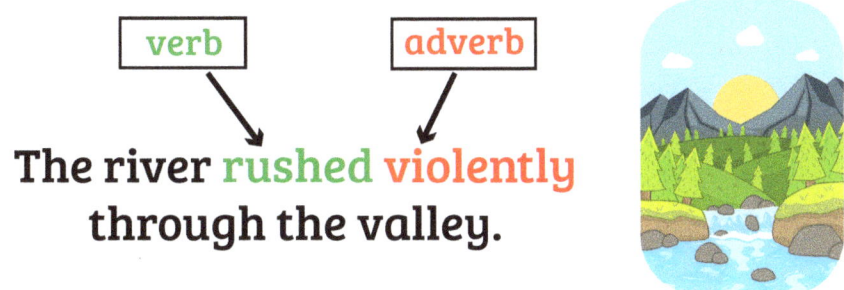

adverbial: A single word (adverb) or group of words (adverbial clause or adverbial phrase) that modifies/gives extra information to the sentence or the verb.

A-Z English Dictionary

adverbial clause: A clause that functions as an adverb. The clause can modify the sentence. There are many different ways a sentence can be modified by an adverbial clause.

Type	Example
Time	After he arrived, Max went straight to sleep.
Place	Wherever there is a dead animal, vultures will gather.
Cause	I ate lunch early because I was hungry.
Contrast	Although Seema woke up late, she got to school on time.
Condition	If you wear a hat, it will keep you warm when it is cold.
Purpose	He went to night school so that he could get a better job.
Result	I ate lunch early because I was hungry.
Manner	The athletes were tired so they ran more slowly than before.

A-Z English Dictionary

adverbial phrase: A group of words that functions as an adverb.

Type	Example
Time	Within seconds the baby fell asleep.
Place	The man, who lives next door, is a pilot.
Purpose	Susan baked a cake for her brother.
Frequency	The children play football every day.
Manner	The carpenter hit the nail with a hammer.

alliteration: Words that start with the same sound (not just letters) and are repeated in a phrase or sentence.

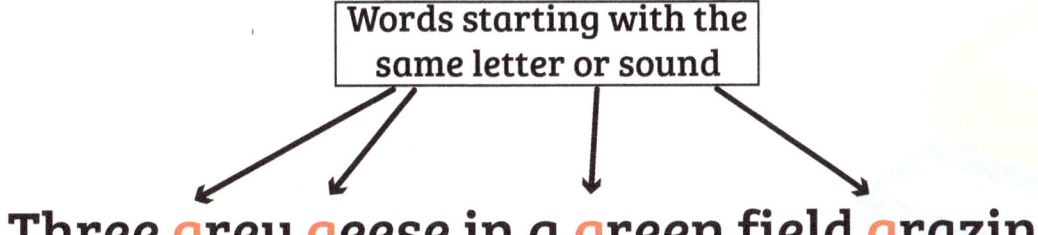

Three grey geese in a green field grazing.

(Words starting with the same letter or sound)

A-Z English Dictionary

alphabet: A set of letters or symbols used to represent the sounds of a language.

Aa Bb Cc Dd Ee Ff Gg Hh Ii Jj Kk Ll Mm

Nn Oo Pp Qq Rr Ss Tt Uu Vv Ww Xx Yy Zz

alphabetical order: Organising words in order according to the alphabet. If the first letter of words are the same, then they are ordered according to the second letter. If the first two letters are the same, then the words are ordered according to the third letter and so on.

First letter
Second letter
Third letter

actor dark dive maybe moon mop

antonym: A word whose meaning is the opposite of another word.

hot ⟷ cold

happy ⟷ sad

wet ⟷ dry

A-Z English Dictionary

apostrophe: A punctuation mark that shows contraction 1. or possession 2.

1.

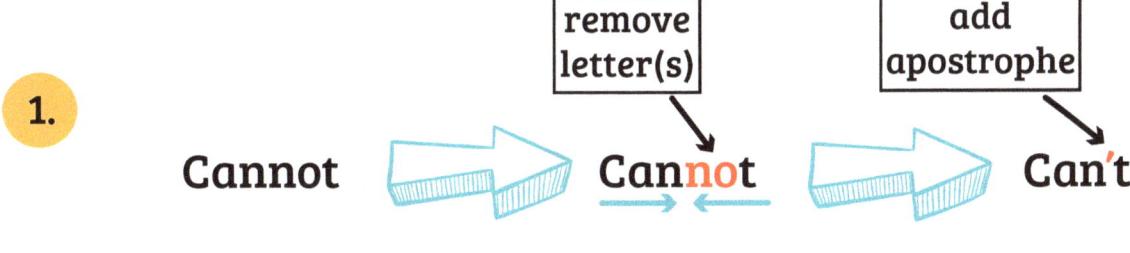

2.

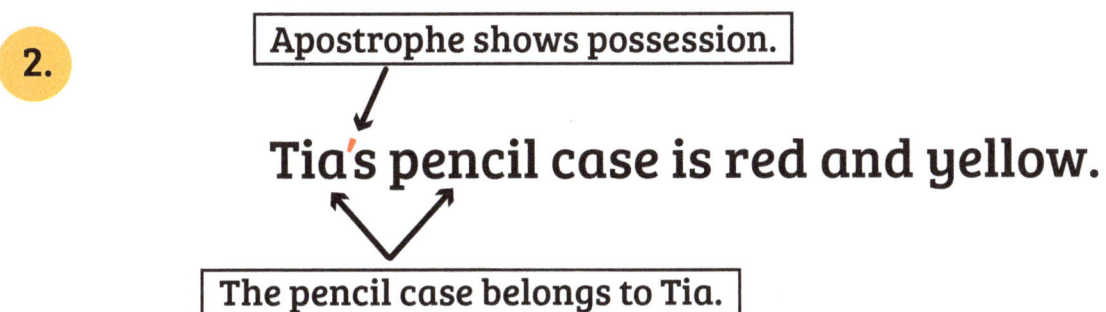

appendix: A section at the end of a book or document that gives extra information about the book it is usually found in non-fiction and reference books.

A-Z English Dictionary

article (i): An article is a word that goes before a noun such as <u>the</u> and <u>a</u>. There are two types of article a) definite article e.g. <u>the</u>   b) indefinite article e.g. <u>a</u>

<u>a) definite article</u> - this word is used when the previous sentence gives you a small clue or information about the next sentence you are writing.

> The previous sentence gives the reader information about where I went.

I went swimming with my friends.
The swimming pool was very crowded.

> Definite article 'the' is used.

<u>b) indefinite article</u> - This word is used when there are no clues in previous sentences and the noun is being introduced for the first time.

A swimming pool is a good place to get some exercise.

> Indefinite article 'a' is used

A-Z English Dictionary

article (ii): A piece of writing that is included with other pieces of writing in a publication such as a newspaper or magazine.

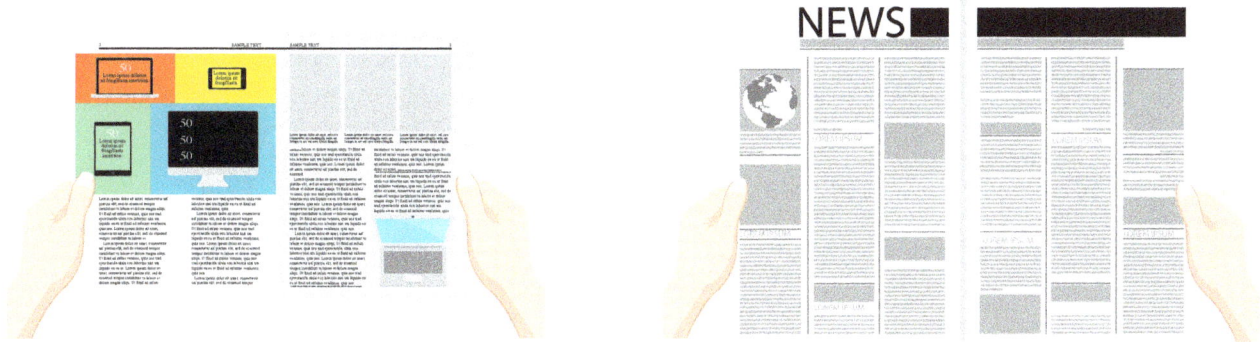

ascender : Letters that rise above the main body of the letter. e.g. h, b, d.

assonance : The repeated use of a vowel sound in writing. Often used in poetry and rap music to create a specific effect.

I m**a**de my w**a**y to the b**a**ke s**a**le.

atmosphere : The way a writer uses words and description to create certain feelings for the reader.

A-Z English Dictionary

audience: The specific group of people you are writing for. When writing a text, the audience would be the people who are most likely to read the text.

autobiography: An account written by someone about his or her own life.

auxiliary verb: Auxiliary verbs are often called 'helping verbs,' and are used together with the main verb to show the verb's tense or to make it into a negative sentence or question.

present tense/past tense

To be	To have	To do
I am/was	I have/had	I do/did
you are/were	you have/had	you do/did
he is/was	he has/had	he does/did
she is/was	she has/had	she does/did
it is/was	it has/had	it does/did
you are/were	you have/had	you do/did
we are/were	we have/had	we do/did
they are/were	they have/had	they do/did

A-Z English Dictionary

bilingual: Able to speak two languages fluently.

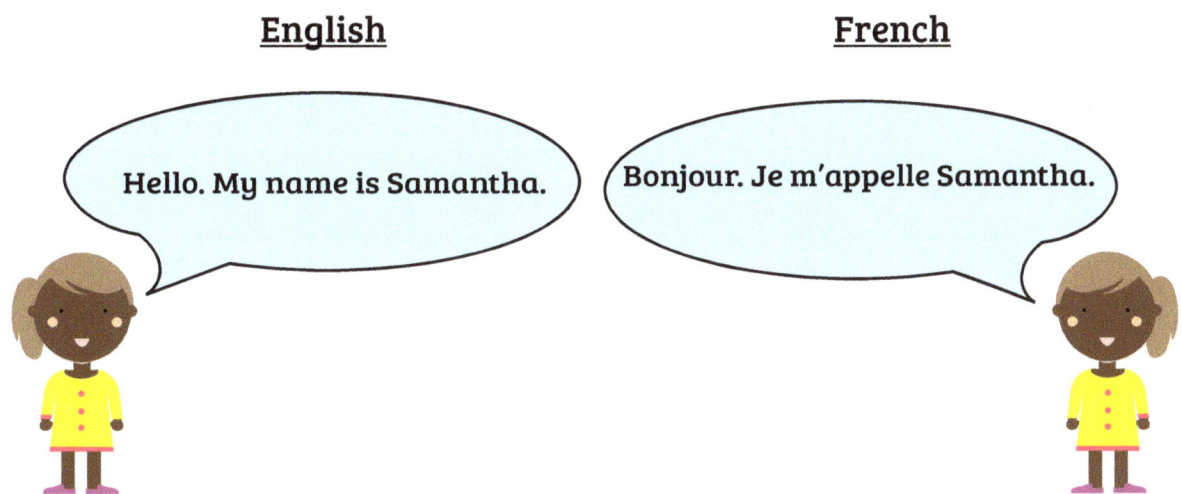

biliterate: Able to write two languages.

biography: The story of one person's life written by another person.

blurb: A short description of a book written in a way to entice the person reading the blurb to buy and read the book. The blurb is often found written on the back cover of the book.

A-Z English Dictionary

bold: Text that is made thicker and darker so that it stands out from the page and grabs the reader's attention.

brackets: A pair of punctuation marks that are placed around words giving extra information to a sentence. It is not essential to the meaning of the sentence.

Mount Everest (in the Himalayas) is the tallest mountain in the world.

browse: To casually look through a text or book.

browser: A piece of computer software that is used to access the internet.

bullet point: A punctuation mark in the form of a black circle used to show each new part of a list.

• bullet point

calligram: A word, piece of text or a poem in which the design and layout of the letters create a visual image that relates to the text.

A-Z English Dictionary

capital letter: The upper case of a letter. It should be used in a number of ways.

i) At the start of names of people, places or words relating to them.

Person/Place	Related words
Bhuddha	**B**huddhism
India	**I**ndian

ii) At the beginning of a sentence.

It often snows during the winter.

iii) In the title of books, movies, organisations and special days.

Harry **P**otter and the **P**risoner of **A**zkaban.
The **U**nited **N**ations.
New **Y**ear's **D**ay.

iv) In abbreviations.

USA (**U**nited **S**tates of **A**merica)

FIFA (**F**ederation **I**nternationale **F**ootball **A**ssociation)

UNICEF (**U**nited **N**ations **I**nternational **C**hildren's **E**mergency **F**und)

A-Z English Dictionary

caption: A small description that goes with an illustration or photograph. Captions are often found in non-fiction books.

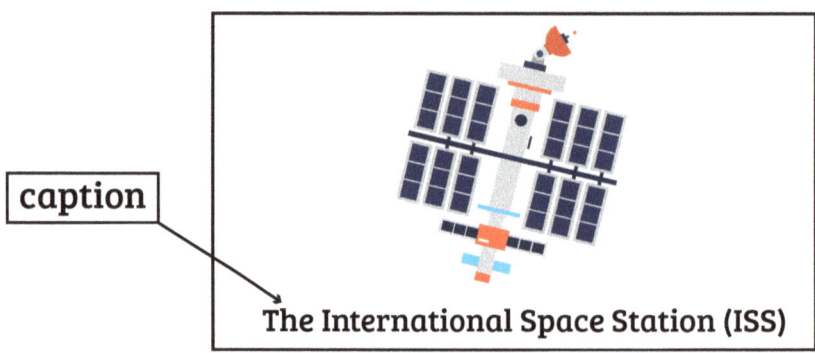

chapter: The main division of a book, usually with a title or number.

character: A person or other (e.g. animal, robot) that appears in a story. A character can be entirely made up or based around a real person. A character often guides the reader through the story, helping the reader understand the plot.

Well known characters

Shrek   Olaf   Harry Potter

A-Z English Dictionary

characterisation: The process by which the author reveals the personality of a character.

i) <u>Direct Characterisation.</u> - The author describes a character by telling the reader what the character is thinking and feeling.

Riku was so angry he shouted at his friends.

ii) <u>Indirect Characterisation.</u> - The author shows the reader how a character is thinking and feeling without telling the reader. This is often called 'show not tell.' Show not tell can be done in a number of ways:

Speech	"No I won't share my ball, you can't play with me!" yelled Riku.	By yelling at his friends and not sharing his ball, the reader knows Riku is angry.
Thoughts	Unsure why he yelled, Riku turned his back towards the others.	This tells the reader that Riku is not angry with his friends, but angry about something else.
Effect on others	Surprised, the children decided to play elsewhere and leave him to calm down.	The way his friends have acted continues to tell the reader that Riku is angry.
Actions	Riku gripped his ball tightly, holding it for comfort.	The reader now knows that Riku is upset and not angry. Holding the ball tells you he is sad.
Looks	His red face started to fade as he stared into the distance.	Riku is starting to calm down but staring in the distance lets the reader know that he is still upset and the problem will be revisited later in the story.

A-Z English Dictionary

checklist: Sometimes called success criteria. A list of criteria against which achievements can be measured.

chronological: In time order. When something is described as chronological, it will have been ordered according to time.

A school day - In chronological order.

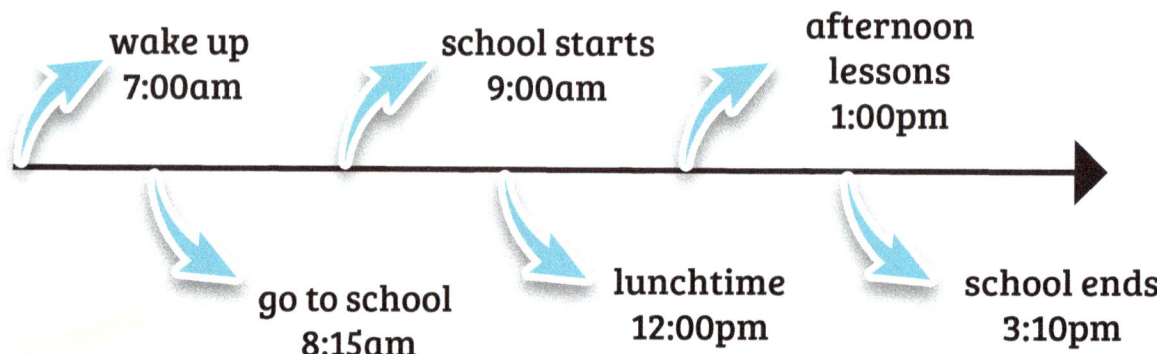

A-Z English Dictionary

cinquain: A short poem made up of five usually non-rhyming lines. In total the cinquin has 22 syallables that are organised as a sequence 2 , 4 , 6 , 8 , 2.

>Desserts (2)
>sweet and tasty (4)
>eat them after mealtimes (6)
>or when nobody is watching (8)
>naughty (2)

clause: A set of words containing a verb. (See main clause and independent clause.)

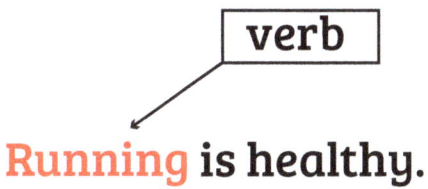

Running is healthy.

clerihew: A humerous poem of four lines, with the first/second, third/fourth lines rhyming. A clerihew is about the person named in the first line.

My teacher, Miss Potts	(A)
Really can talk lots.	(A)
She jibber jabbers all day long	(B)
And many times breaks into song.	(B)

A-Z English Dictionary

climax: The turning point and most intense part of a story. Usually the main character or characters of a story come face to face with the problems that have been building up over the story.

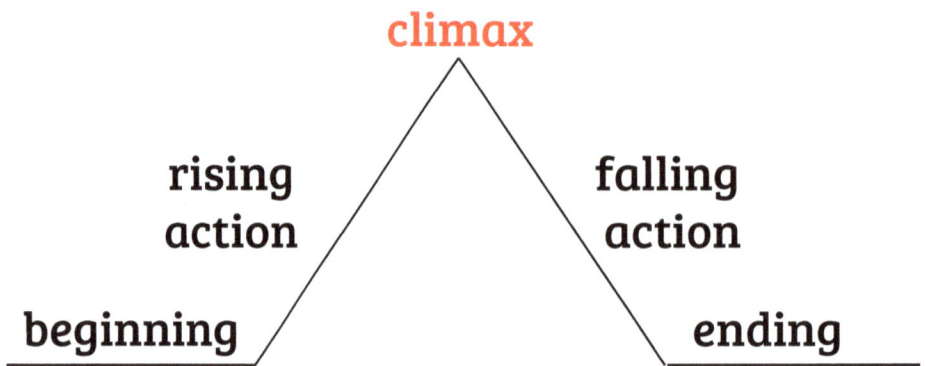

cloze: A procedure where words are left out and the reader can choose the correct word so that it makes sense.

cloze procedure

orbit satellite moon

A _____ is a _____ that in _____ around a planet.

A-Z English Dictionary

collective noun: A type of noun that is used to name a group of things. It can be items, people or animals.

a forest of trees   a team of players   a gaggle of geese

colloquial: Language used in everyday speech. It is usually informal and can sometimes be called slang.

pal / mate = friend
cash = money
gimme = give to me

colon: A punctuation mark (:) that can be used to introduce a list or to add further detail .

1. Introduces a list

I saw the following animals at the zoo: lions, tigers and penguins.

2. A De:De sentence has two parts

The 1st part gives a description.

The tiger is a fierce creature: it attacks its prey by using sharp claws and razor sharp teeth.

The 2nd part gives further details.

A-Z English Dictionary

comma: A punctuation mark that can be used to mark between items in a list or to mark pauses between clauses in a sentence.

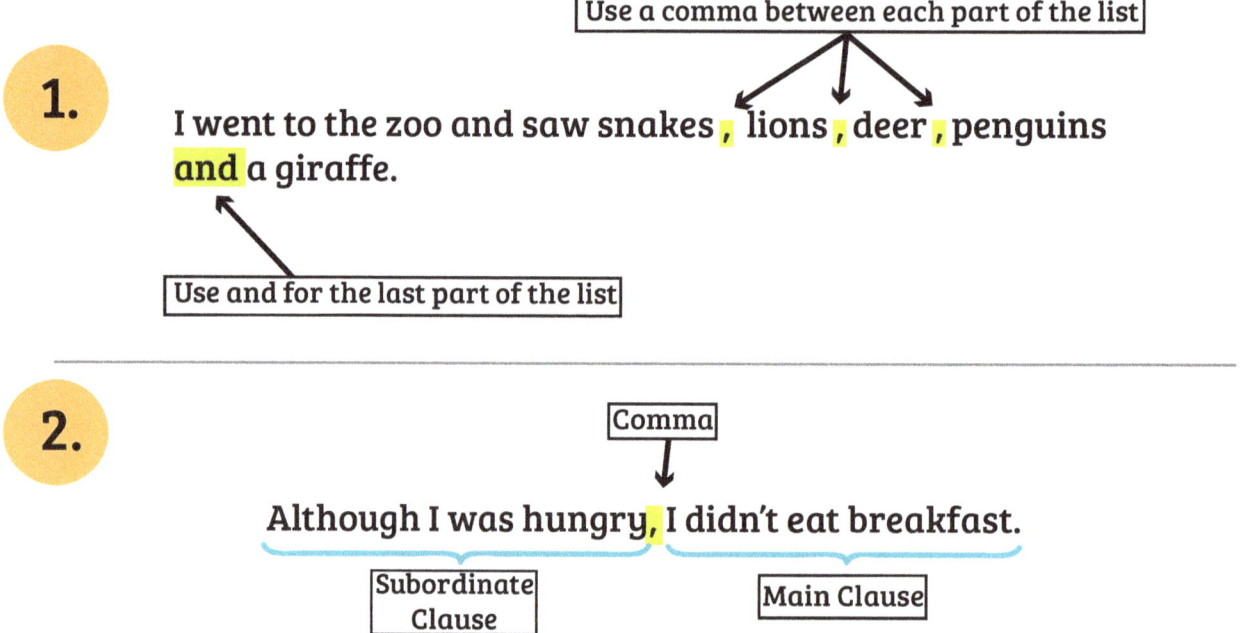

1. I went to the zoo and saw snakes, lions, deer, penguins and a giraffe.
   - Use a comma between each part of the list
   - Use and for the last part of the list

2. Although I was hungry, I didn't eat breakfast.
   - Subordinate Clause / Main Clause / Comma

command: A sentence that demands or asks that something is done.

Go to the shop and get me some milk. - **command**

common noun: A name given to a common thing.

table   mountain   teacher

A-Z English Dictionary

communication: A two-way process of exchanging information and opinions through speech, listening and reading.

comparative adjective: Adjectives used to compare differences between two different objects. Can use either the suffix 'er' or the words more/most.

<u>one-syllable adjectives (in almost all cases)</u>

big	bigger
small	smaller
thin	thinner

<u>two-syllable adjectives (in many cases)</u>

happy	happier
simple	simpler
narrow	narrower

<u>three-syllable adjectives (use more)</u>

beautiful	more beautiful
difficult	more difficult
expensive	more expensive

<u>irregular adjectives (some don't follow the rules)</u>

good	better
bad	worse
far	further

complex sentence: A sentence with one or more clauses. At a minimum, a complex sentence must have one subordinate clause and one main clause. The order in which the clauses are written can change. Some complex sentences have many clauses.

complex sentence (i)

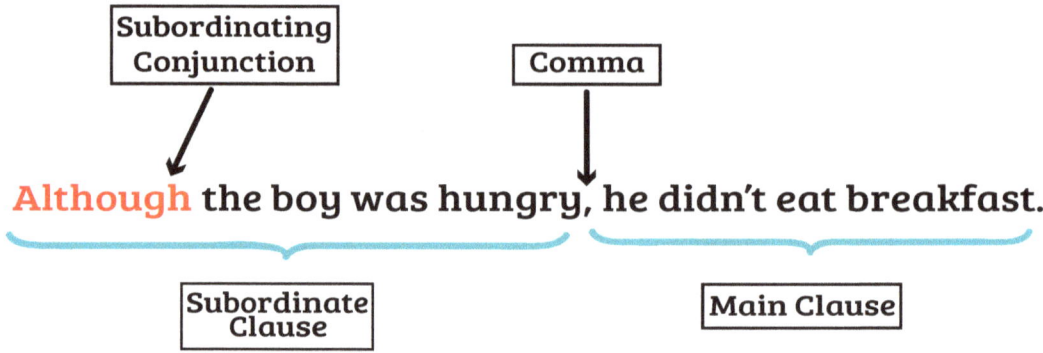

complex sentence (ii)

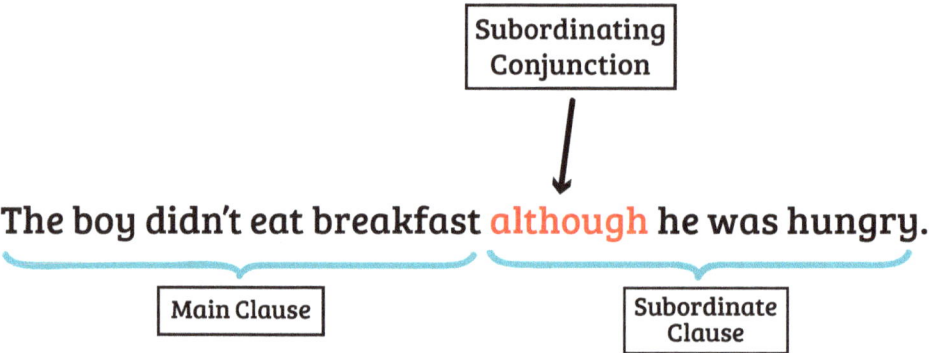

complex sentence (iii) - subordinate clause embedded in the main clause.

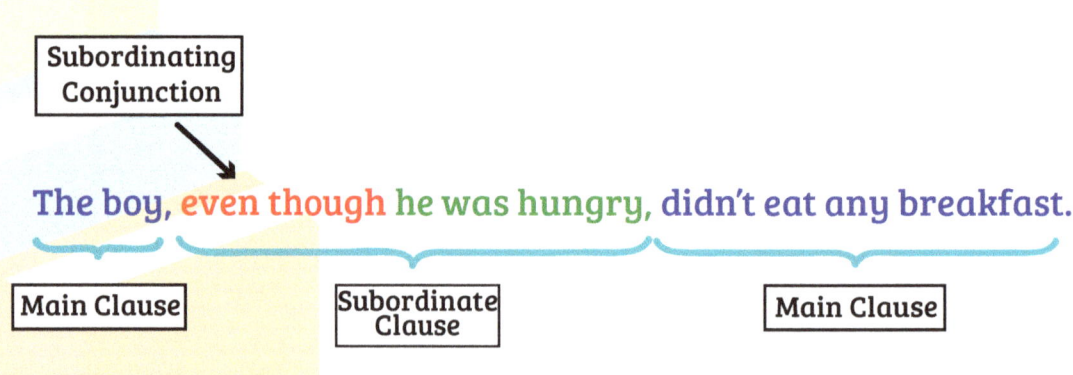

A-Z English Dictionary

compose: To put together a piece of writing. To create and think how a piece of writing should fit together.

composition: A finished piece of writing that has been put together by the author. The whole process involves planning, drafting, editing, redrafting and publication.

compound sentence: A sentence that contains two main clauses which are joined together using a coodinating conjunction.

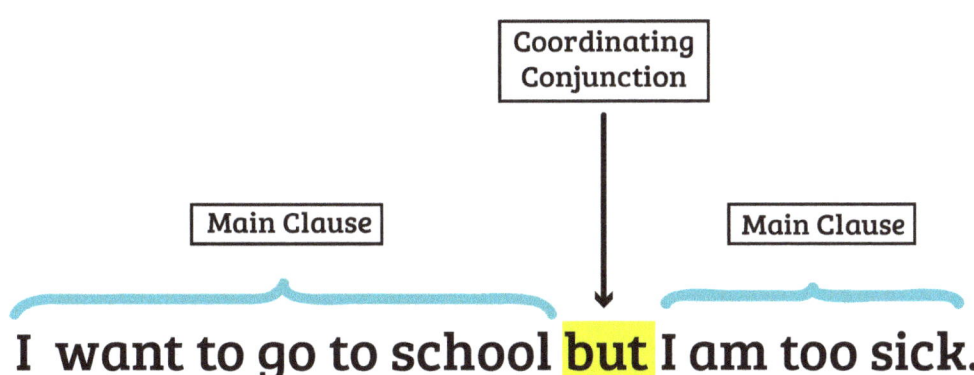

compound word: A word that is made up from two or more words.

closed compound (written as a single word)

snow + man = snowman

basket + ball = basketball

moon + light = moonlight

compound with a hyphen (-)

bad + tempered = bad-tempered

sugar + free = sugar-free

good + looking = good-looking

open compound (two separate words)

school + bus = school bus

dinner + table = dinner table

living + room = living room

A-Z English Dictionary

comprehension: The process of understanding a piece of writing. Comprehension in primary schools is mostly linked with being able to answer different types of questions on a text.

conclusion: The final part of a text that brings it to an end. The conclusion is often linked to the introduction.

concrete noun: A type of noun that can be seen through the five senses of hearing, seeing, touching, smelling and tasting. If you cannot see, hear, touch, smell or taste it, then it is not a concrete noun.

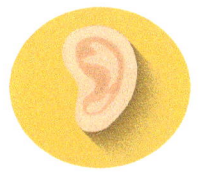 **hear:**   bell   whistle   song

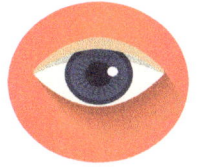 **see:**   mountain   ball   car

 **touch:**   wool   rock   paper

 **smell:**   flower   perfume   cake

 **taste:**   chocolate   cake   apple

A-Z English Dictionary

concrete poem: Sometimes called a 'shape poem'. A concrete poem is designed so that the shape of the poem matches the subject of the poem.

conjunction: A word used to connect clauses within a single sentence. Coordinating conjunctions are used to connect main clauses and form compound sentences. Subordinating conjunctions are used in subordinatate clauses within complex sentences.

coordinating conjunction

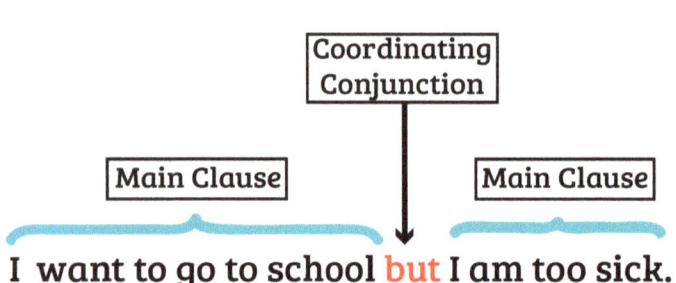

Coordinating Conjunctions
F - for
A - and
N - nor
B - but
O - or
Y - yet
S - so

subordinating conjunction

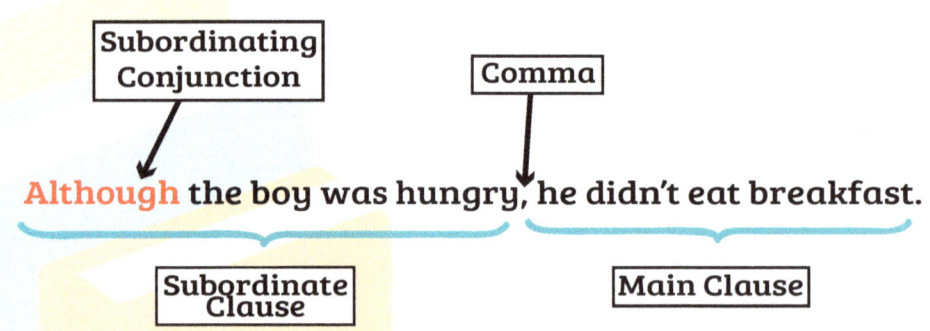

Subordinating Conjunctions
although
until
if
because
where
as

A-Z English Dictionary

connective: A word that is used to link clauses or sentences in order to create continuity.

connectives can be conjunctions or adverbials:

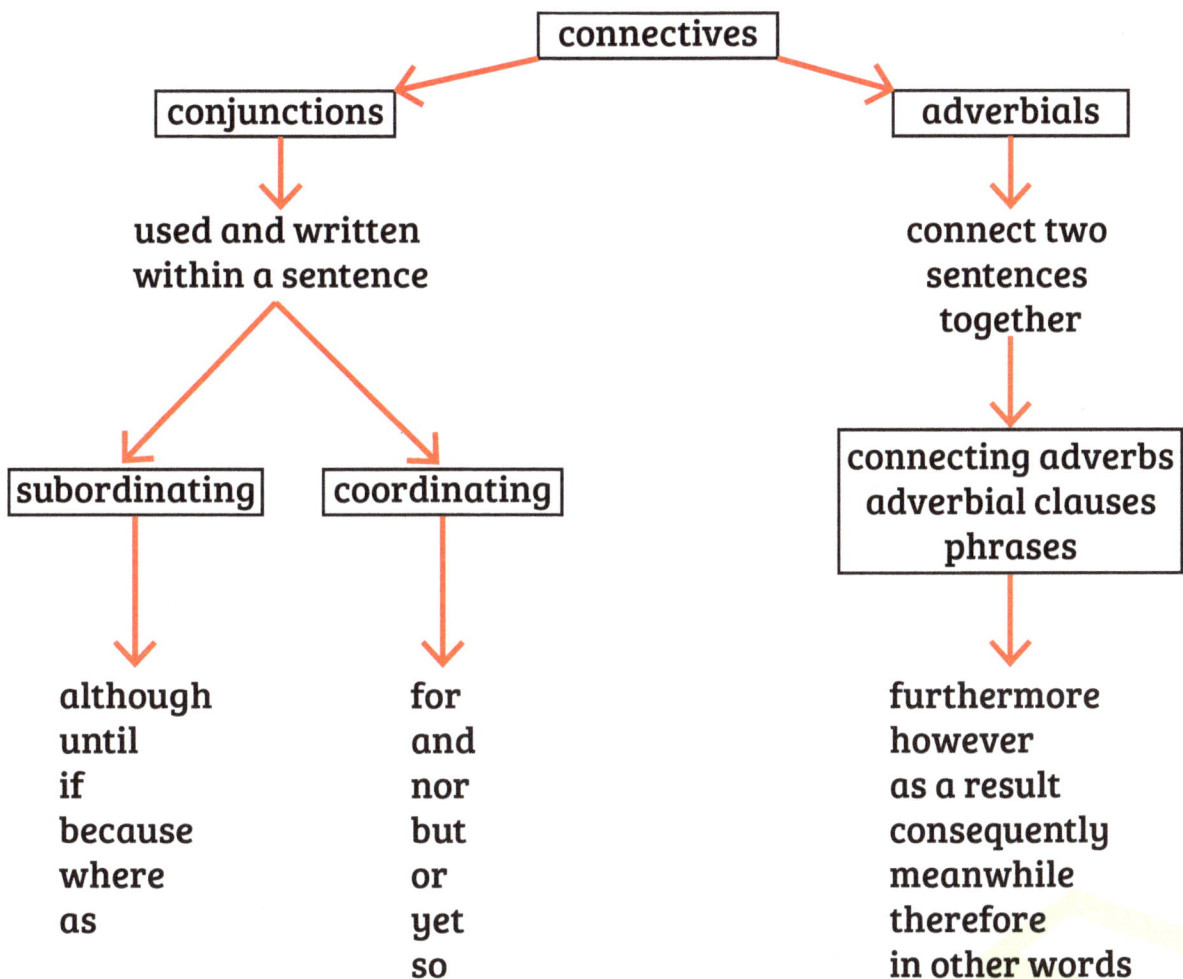

conscience alley: A drama technique that is useful to use when a character is facing a dilemma. It provides an opportunity to see both viewpoints of the problem.

A-Z English Dictionary

consonant: All the letters in the alphabet except vowels.

| consonants | vowels |

Bb Cc Dd Ff Gg Hh Jj Kk Ll Mm

Nn Pp Qq Rr Ss Tt Vv Ww Xx Yy Zz

Aa Ee Ii Oo Uu

contents page: A page at the beginning of a book which tells the reader what is contained in the book and on which page each section begins. Mostly seen in non-fiction books.

contraction A word or two words that are shortened by removing one or more letters and replacing them with an apostrophe.

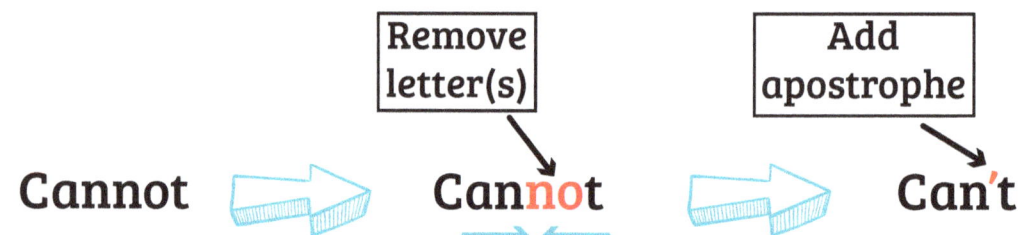

couplet: Two consecutive lines that rhyme. Often used in poetry.

> While I was out walking with my brother Jim,
> somebody threw a tomato at him.

dash: A punctuation mark that can be used instead of brackets or may replace other types of punctuation like commas. A pair of dashes can also separate a strong interruption from the rest of the sentence.

Interruption after the noun:

The building – which is about to collapse – was built hundreds of years ago.

If at the end of a sentence only one dash is used:

They were trapped, there was no other way out – or was there?

debate: A discussion between two people or groups of people who have different opinions and argue for and against an idea.

deduction: (See inference.)

definite article: The word <u>the</u> is a definite article. (See article (i).)

dependent clause: (See subordinate clause.)

descender : Letters that rise below the main body of the letter. e.g. g, y, p.

descriptive language: The use of adjectives to try to create a detailed picture in the mind of the reader. Descriptive language should appeal to the five senses: sight, hearing, smell, touch and taste.

determiner: A word that goes before the noun and identifies the noun even further.

Articles	Demonstrative	Possessive
the an a	this that these those	my its your our his their her

Quantifiers	Question words	Ordinal
many a lot of few any some less	which what whose	first second next last

A-Z English Dictionary

Dewey decimal: A system where non-fiction books are organised into different categories and each category is given a set of numbers. This makes it easier to find non-fiction books in a library

book numbers	subject area	type of books
000 - 099	Information & General Reference	encyclopedias, books with facts, information books
100 - 199	Philosophy & Psychology	books that explain how we think and feel and human behaviour
200 - 299	Religion	books about the different religions around the world
300 - 399	Social Science	books about society celebrations, customs, money, transportation
400 - 499	Language	the different languages around the world
500 - 599	Science	animals, plants, stars and planets, rocks, fossils, habitats, dinosaurs
600 - 699	Technology	cooking, inventions, human body, pets
700 - 799	Arts & Recreation	art, drawings, handicrafts sports, games
800 - 899	Literature	poetry, plays, classical stories, riddles
900 - 999	History & Geography	landforms, travel, exploration, historical events

D

A-Z English Dictionary

diagram: A pictoral representation often found in non-fiction texts. A diagram is clearly labelled and is included to support the reader in understanding the text.

dialect: A form of language that is spoken in a particular area or region. People may speak the same language (e.g. English) but use different words and phrases depending on where they live.

Standard English	Southern U.S.A
How do you do?	Howdy?

Standard English	N.E England
maybe	mebbies

Standard English	N. Ireland
Let's go for a walk.	Let's go for a dander.

dialogue: A conversation between two or more people.

A-Z English Dictionary

dictionary: A reference book that lists words in alphabetical order and explains their meaning. A dictionary can focus on specific categories e.g. English and Mathematics.

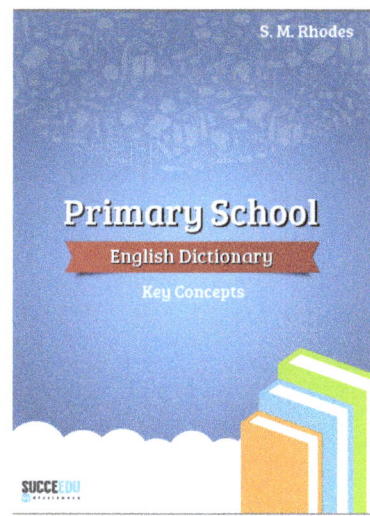 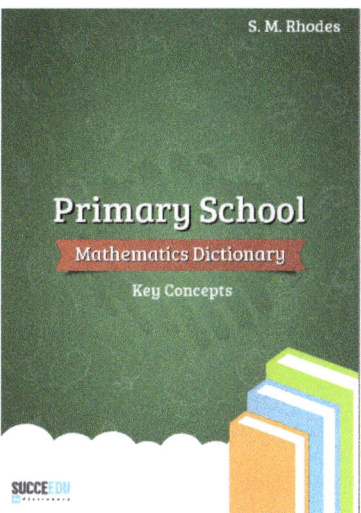

direct speech: Words that are spoken by someone. They come directly out of the person's mouth and are written using speech marks.

direct speech

" I am going out for dinner tonight," said the boy .

I am going out for dinner tonight.

discussion text: A piece of writing that discusses both viewpoints of a particular problem. Both viewpoints should be balanced and the text should not deliberately persuade the reader to choose a viewpoint.

A-Z English Dictionary

double negative: Two negative words or phrases used in the same sentence. Two negatives actually cancel each other out and make it positive. This can be very confusing and so are discouraged from being used.

double negative	meaning
I don't want nothing.	If you don't want nothing, you must want something.
We haven't never seen a lion.	If you haven't never seen a lion, then you must have actually seen one.

draft: To write a text before writing a final copy. A writer can edit and draft as many copies as they like until they are ready to publish.

drama strategy: Techniques used to explore an issue, a character or a text. Popular strategies include conscience alley, hot-seating, role-play and thought-tracking.

edit: To change and improve a draft before publishing. Editing includes: checking spellings, checking punctuation, changing words for a better effect and making sure the text makes sense.

A-Z English Dictionary

ellipsis: A punctuation mark (…) also called the suspension or omission mark. It has two main uses.

i) suspension or hesitation -

Slowly he crept forward and opened the door…
I… don't… know… what to do.

ii) omission - leaving out words that may not be important.

Today, after thinking for a while, we decided not to go.
Today … we decided not to go.

empathy: An emotional response where one person puts themselves in the position of another person or character. Empathy can be used when the reader tries to understand from a character's perspective.

encode: The process of using letter sounds when attempting to spell a word. (See decode.)

encyclopedia: A book or set of books that give information on many different subjects. Each subject is ordered in alphabetical order.

evaluation: Judging and discussing the quality of a text based on a set of criteria. The criteria should include all the elements that make a text a success. You can evaluate alone (self-assessment) with a class mate (peer assessment) or with the teacher.

exclamation mark: A punctuation mark (!) that is used to show feelings of surprise, anger or joy.

Surprise: Thats amazing!

Anger: Stop it!

Joy: I am so happy!

A-Z English Dictionary

explanation: A type of text whose purpose is to explain how something works or explain the process of a natural phenomenon such as day and night.

expressive reading: Reading a text with feeling so that it matches what has been written. To be able to use expression, the reader must understand the words and the sentence structures of the text.

fable: A short story that contains a moral or lesson. Fables often use animals or inanimate objects as the main characters.

Fable	Moral
The Tortoise and the Hare	Don't brag and show off.
The Boy Who Cried Wolf	Don't lie otherwise people won't believe you.
The Ant and the Grasshopper	Be responsible for yourself.

fact: Something that is proved to be true.

fairy tale: A traditional story written for children that is set in the past. Usually involves magical creatures such as fairies, wizards, wiches and goblins.

Cinderella

Goldilocks and The Three Bears

fantasy: A narrative story that is far removed from normal reality. Fantasy stories often include unusual characters and an element of magic and can take place in magical lands.

Chronicles of Narnia: The Lion, The Witch and The Wardrobe

A-Z English Dictionary

fiction: A story or piece of writing that is based on the imagination and not necessarily on facts. A fictional story does not claim to be telling a true story.

figurative language: A way to use words, sentences and phrases to suggest meaning and to create mental images for the reader. There is some disagreement as to how many kinds of figurative language there are. Below is a list of five of the main types.

Simile: The carpet was as thick as a layer of freshly fallen snow.

Metaphor: The moon is a shining pearl.

Personification: The sun smiled upon the children playing on the beach below.

Onamatopoeia: The river crashed and smashed its way past the rocks.

folk tale: A story that has been passed down from generation to generation. Generally a folk tale was told orally through story telling. However today, many folk tales are printed in books.

A-Z English Dictionary

font: A set of letters and numbers of the same style.

>   **font - Bree Serif**
>   font - Ariel
>   font – Chalkboard

formal language: Language that is used in more serious situations. An example could be writing a persuasive letter to the headteacher. Formal language does not use contractions or slang language.

freeze frame: Like pressing the pause button on a T.V., freeze framing is a drama strategy that can be used in English lessons to discuss a character's thoughts and feelings at a particular moment in time.

full stop: A punctuation mark that marks the end of a sentence.

A-Z English Dictionary

future tense: A tense that describes what will happen in the future.

i) Future tense verbs do not have their own endings. Instead they use present tense verbs with extra information.

> He goes shopping on Monday.
> He is going shopping on Monday.

ii) Or with an auxiliary verb.

> He will go shopping on Monday.

genre: Texts that share the same characteristics are said to belong to the same group or genre.

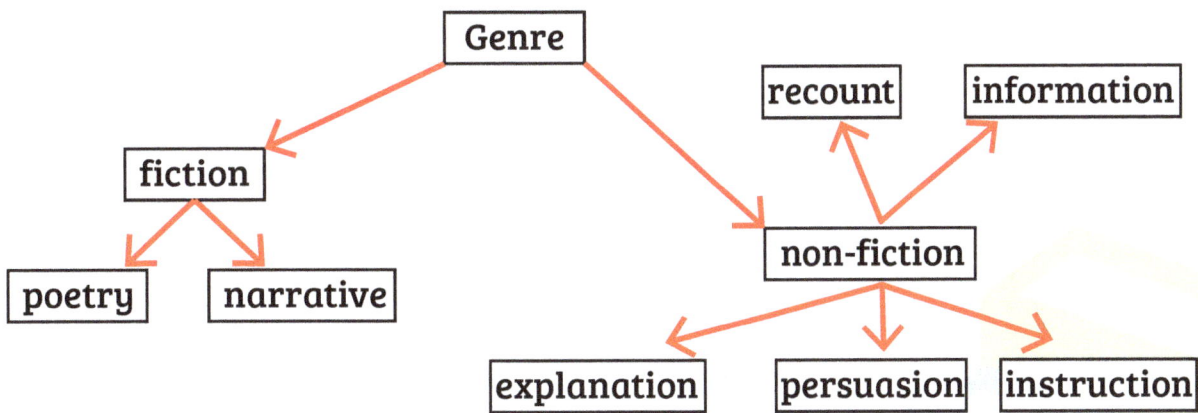

A-Z English Dictionary

gesture: A non-verbal way to communicate feelings, mood and opinion. Gesture is mostly done by the head and hands although other parts of the body can be used.

glossary: An alphabetical list found at the back of a book that explains the meaning of words that are highlighted or typed in bold within the book.

grammar: The rules for constructing sentences.

guided reading: A way to be a better reader and understand a text in more detail by studying in a small group of classmates and a teacher.

A-Z English Dictionary

haiku: . A Japanese poem of three lines made up of 5, 7 and 5 syllables.

    Line 1: 5 syllables   The sky is so blue
    Line 2: 7 syllables   Flowers bloom and petals sway
    Line 3: 5 syllables   It's a summer's day

heading: Another word for title. Written at the top of a page and used to introduce what will follow underneath.

high frequency words: Words that are written and used most often.

highlighting: Marking a text to make certain words, phrases or sentences stand out. Highlighting can be done for reasons such as: editing, searching for word types and peer assessing.

    This is a highlighted word.

home language: The language that is spoken the most amongst family.

A-Z English Dictionary

homograph: Two words that have the same spellings, the same or different pronunciation but have different meanings.

tear - to shed a tear

tear - to rip

bat - sports equipment

bat - flying mammal

homonym: Two words that have the same or different spellings, the same pronunciation but have different meanings.

see - to look

sea - the ocean

pear - fruit

pair - two

A-Z English Dictionary

homophone: Two words with different spellings, are pronounced the same but have different meanings.

<u>hair</u> - on one's head

<u>hare</u> - rabbit-like animal

<u>pain</u> - suffering

<u>pane</u> - plate of glass

horror: A genre of fiction where the stories are supposed to frighten, scare or disgust the reader.

hot seat: A drama strategy that involves questioning a person or group of people who are acting in role. Hot seating helps gain a deeper understanding of a character's thoughts and feelings.

A-Z English Dictionary

hyphen: A punctuation mark used to join some compound words.

bad + tempered = bad-tempered
sugar + free = sugar-free
good + looking = good-looking

idiom: A phrase or sentence that has a very different meaning from the words themselves .

Idiom	Meaning	Example
Piece of cake	when something is very easy to do	Running two miles was a piece of cake.
Spill the beans	telling a secret	"Don't spill the beans, the party is a surprise."
Feeling blue	feeling sad	People can feel blue when the weather is cold.

illustration: A picture in a story book is called an illustration.

illustrator: The person who draws the pictures in a book. Quentin Blake is a famous illustrator.

image: A picture that represents an object or person.

imagery: Words used in a text that help the reader create a picture in their mind.

indefinite article: The words 'a' and 'an' are indefinite articles. (See article (i).)

indefinite pronoun: A pronoun that does not refer to a place, a person or thing.

singular examples		plural examples	
anybody	somebody	both	several
anything	something	many	few
anyone	someone	others	fewer

independent clause: A clause that will stand on its own. (See main clause.)

independent activities: Activites that are carried out by oneself and with little or no adult support.

index: An alphabetically ordered list found in the back of a book. The list tells the reader on which page or pages they would find specific words in the text.

indirect speech: Also called reported speech. Indirect speech is speech that is reported by a second person and certain grammatical changes have to be made to the sentence.

Today is my birthday!

indirect speech

He said that today was his birthday.

inference: (Inference and deduction are very similar and so will be explained together). Inference or deduction is when the meaning of a text is revealed by the clues from within the text. Things may not be told to you directly, but there are many clues in the writing.

Text	Question	Inference
A man was wearing bright yellow trousers, a red wig and a red nose.	Who was the man?	From the text, the clues tell us the man is a clown.
Mrs Bucket was sniffing and coughing when she called to say she wasn't coming into work that day.	Why did Mrs Bucket not go into work?	From the text, the clues tell us that Mrs Bucket is not well and called in sick.

information text: A non-fiction text written with the purpose of giving the reader information about a specific subject. Diagrams, photographs and a glossary are often included to help the reader understand.

instruction text: A non-fiction text written with the purpose of telling the reader how to do something or how to make something such as bake a cake, make a Christmas card or play a game.

internal rhyme: A rhyme that occurs within a line of text. Three types of internal rhyme are shown below.

i) Two or more rhyming words in the same line

> There was a cat who was quite fat.

ii) Two or more rhyming words in the middle of two or more lines

> On the boat it was quite cold.
> I wore my coat, a hat and scarf.

i) A word at the end of a line rhymes with words in the next line.

> Sitting with friend on a log.
> Along came my dog with a stick.

introduction: The opening paragraph that introduces a text. In fiction, a typical introduction may include the setting, action or character description. In non-fiction an introduction may include a rhetorical question and discuss what the text will be about.

inverted comma: A punctuation mark that is used to show direct speech. Also called speech marks.

" "
...

irregular: Words forms (e.g. nouns and verbs) that do not follow regular spelling rules.

<u>Nouns</u> - singular/plural   <u>Verbs</u> - present/past

tooth / teeth   I go / I went

person / people   I eat / I ate

man / men   I fall / I fell

italic: A font of printed text where the letters slant forward.

This text is typed in italic and slants forward.

jingle: A short rhyming verse that is accompanied with music and is often used in advertisements.

journal (i): Similar to a diary in that it is a factual account of daily events.

journal (ii): A magazine that reports on things of special interest.

kenning: A two word phrase used to describe a person or object. Kennings can also be used to form kenning poems.

<u>My Pet</u>

Paw - licker
Milk - slurper
Ball - chaser
Tail - wagger
Stroke - lover

key: A list of symbols and their meanings which help the reader to understand those symbols when placed on a map or graph. Like a key unlocking a door, a key can unlock the information presented.

A-Z English Dictionary

keyword: Important words that help the reader understand a text. Keywords also help the reader to summarise a text or to do their own further research.

kinaesthetic learning: A learning style where the learning takes place by carrying out physical activities. Learners of this style enjoy using their hands to learn.

label: The writing on a diagram that names the different parts.

layout: The way in which the different parts of a text are placed together. e.g. in non-fiction the paragraphs, diagrams and titles

legend: A heroic story set in the past that has some true and some untrue parts. A legend has important meaning and symbolism to the culture from which it originates.

letter string: A group of letters that appear in a word and are pronounced as one sound.

Letter strings

str - **str**eet
tion - sta**tion**

A-Z English Dictionary

library skills: The knowledge and skills that a person is able to use when searching for books and information in a library. (See Dewey decimal.)

limerick: A funny poem of five lines that can sometimes be silly and make no sense. A limerick has an AABBA rhyming pattern.

Limerick

There was a young man from Darjeeling.
Who jumped up and down on the ceiling.
He had juice up his nose,
and all on his clothes,
because of the orange he was peeling.

literature: Writing such as poems and stories which are thought to be very good and have long-lasting importance to individuals and society.

lower case: Letters of the alphabet which are not capital letters.

Aa Bb Cc Dd Ee Ff Gg Hh Ii Jj Kk Ll Mm

Nn Oo Pp Qq Rr Ss Tt Uu Vv Ww Xx Yy Zz

main clause: A main clause contains a subject and a verb. It makes sense on its own and can also be called an independent clause.

Main clause with subject and verb

Subject — carries out the action

Verb — the action

My sister and I are playing.

Main clause with subject, verb and object

Subject — carries out the action

Verb — the action

Object

My sister and I are playing in the park.

metacognition: Being aware of your own learning and thought processes.

metaphor: Figurative language that is used to compare two things that are not alike but do have things in common.

Mr Snape is a mean dragon.

mime: Acting out a character or in role without saying words and only using gesture and body language.

mind-map: A visual representation of information. It is a good way to organise information about a particular subject.

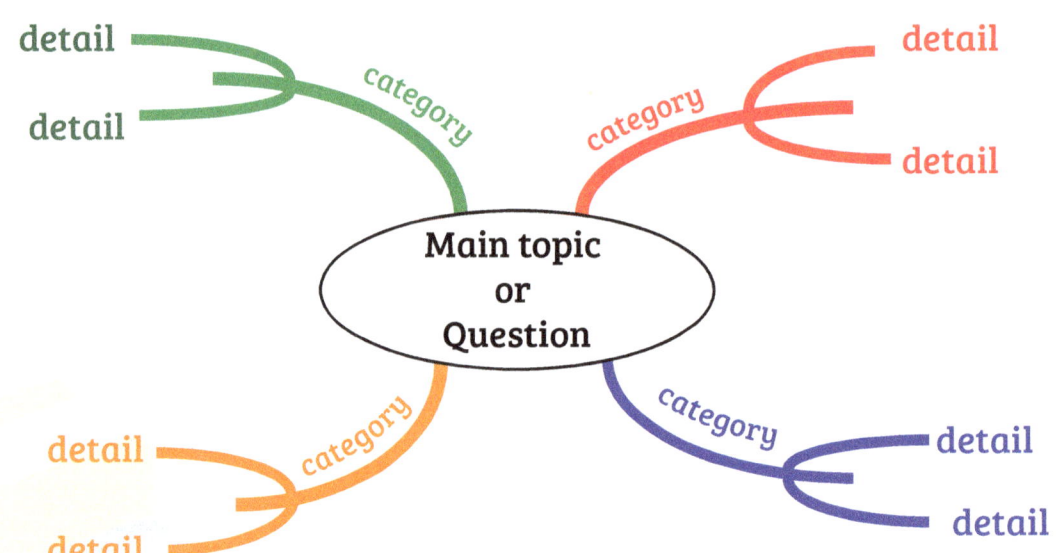

A-Z English Dictionary

misconception: A view or opinion that is incomplete or misunderstood.

mnemonic: A learning strategy that can be used to help remember and recall information. Often can be a word or rhyme thats helps the person to remember.

Mnemonic for the colours of the rainbow

R ichard	Red
O f	Orange
Y ork	Yellow
G ained	Green
B attle	Blue
I n	Indigo
V ain	Violet

modal: A special type of verb that is used to show the level of possibility, necessity or permission.

Positive	Negative
will	will not (won't)
can	cannot (can't)
should	should not (shouldn't)
must	must not (mustn't)
might	might not (mightn't)
would	would not (wouldn't)
could	could not (couldn't)
may	may not

A-Z English Dictionary

mode: The way in which people communicate such as speaking or writing.

modelling: A teaching strategy where the expert will demonstrate how to do something. The expert will also talk out loud and reveal their thoughts. This helps the learner understand the whole process.

modify: Changing the meaning of a word, phrase or clause by making it more precise or specific.

Word type	Word	Modifying word
noun	man	good man
verb	run	run slowly

monolingual: Able to speak only one language.

monologue: A long speech given by one person in a play.

A-Z English Dictionary

monosyllabic: A word that has one syllable.

Monosyllabic words

dog
cat
map
pick

mood: (See atmosphere.)

moral: A message or lesson learned that is often told in a story.

mother tongue: The language that is spoken at home.

multicultural: The ideas and beliefs of many people from different cultures and countries.

multilingual: A person who can speak many languages is described as being multilingual.

multimedia: Using several ways to share information (e.g. video, images, speaking, writing and sounds) to inform and entertain the audience.

myth: A heroic story where the main characters face gods, mythical creatures and monsters. Many myths date back to ancient times and talk about complicated things such as how the Earth was formed or why there is evil in the world.

narrative: A story or an account of events that are told in chronological order. A narrative will have a beginning, middle and ending and can also be told in poem form.

narrator: The person who tells the story is called a narrator. If the narrator is also the participant in the story (e.g. the main character), it is called first-person narrative. If the narrator is not in the actual story, it is called a third-person narrative.

narrative viewpoint: The viewpoint from which a story is written.

non-chronological: When something is non-chronological, sections are put together without being in time order.

non-fiction: Texts that contain facts and information. Instructions, explanations and reports are examples of non-fiction texts.

non-verbal communication: Using the body through facial expression and gesture to communicate thoughts and feelings.

Facial expression   Gesture

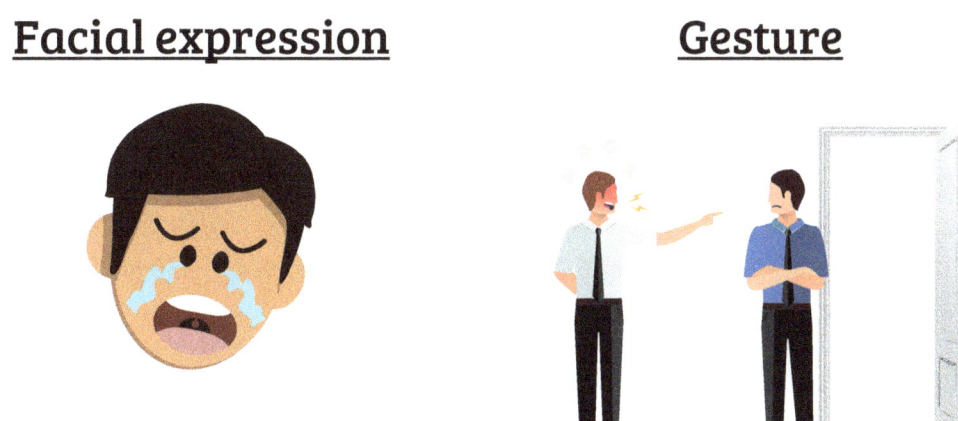

note-taking: The process of writing down the important parts of a text, video or instructions so that you can remember later on.

A-Z English Dictionary

noun: A word that names a person, place, object or idea.

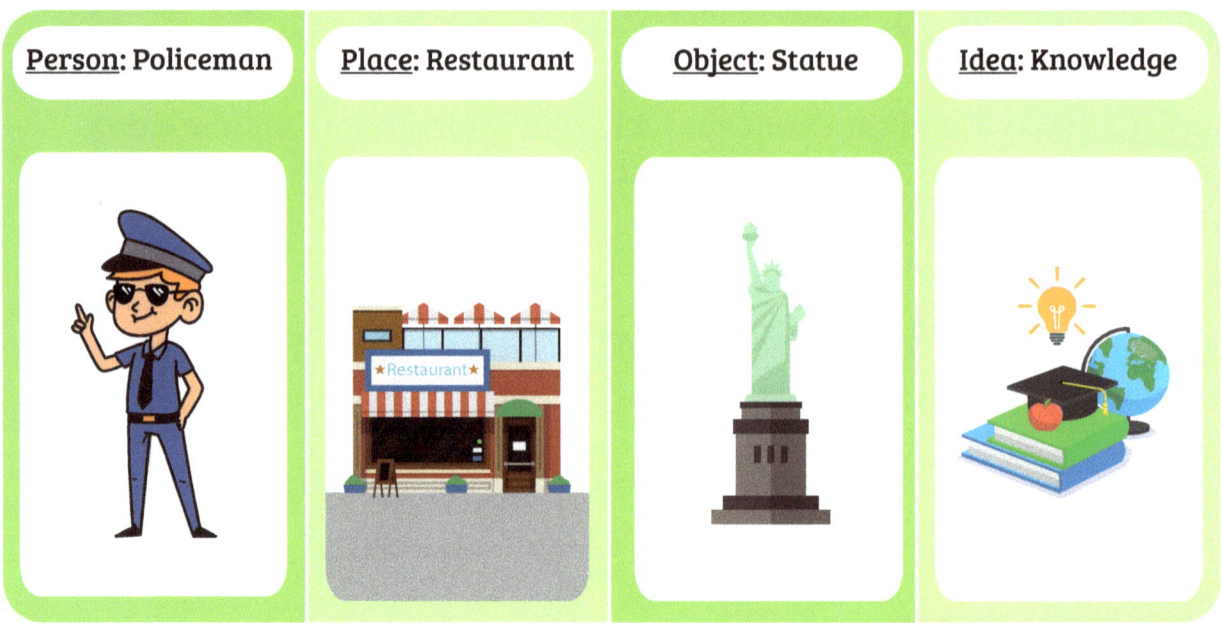

noun phrase: A noun phrase always includes a noun or pronoun. The extra information that modifies the noun is what makes it into a noun phrase.

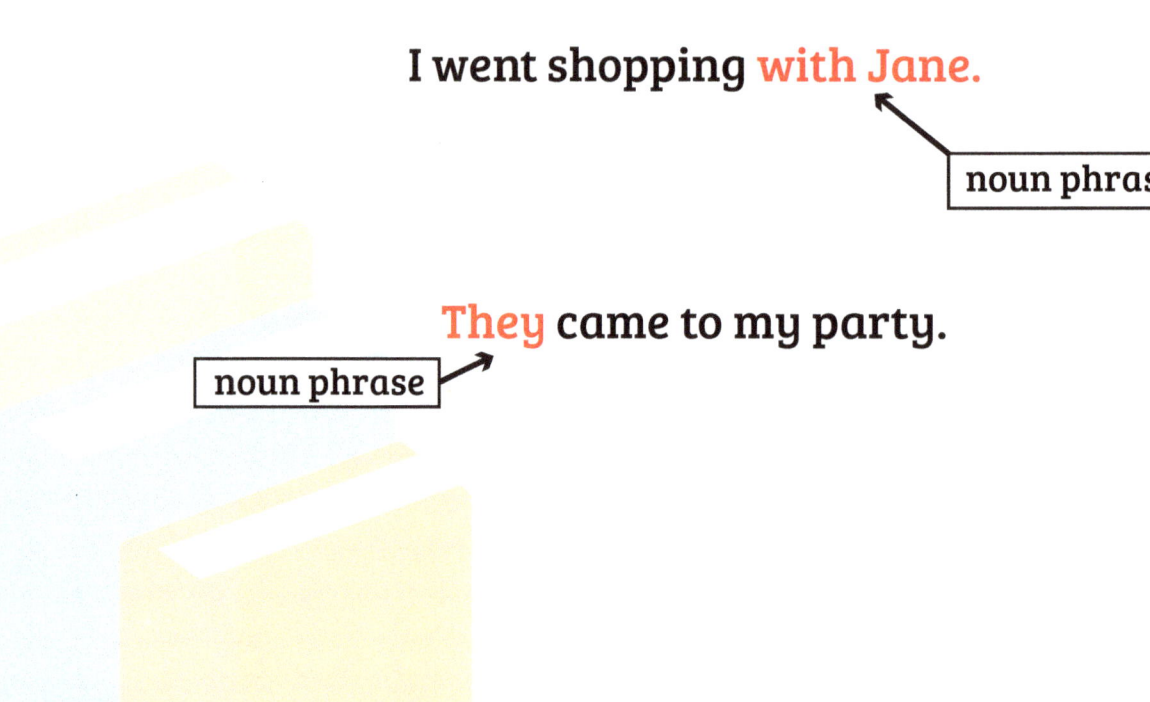

novel: A long fictional story written in chapters.

obituary: A brief biography of someone who has recently died.

object: In grammar, the object is the person or thing that has been acted upon by the subject.

Subject	Verb	Object
carries out the action	the action	

My sister and I are playing in the park.

Subject — carries out the action

Luke wore gloves and a jacket.

Object

Verb — the action

onomatopoeia: A word that when read mimics the sound it is describing.

palindrome: A word, phrase or sentence that reads the same when read forwards or backwards.

racecar

step on no pets

parable: A short story that teaches a moral or spiritual lesson.

paragraph: A section of writing in a larger piece of text. A paragraph is made up of a few sentences about a particular topic or theme.

parentheses: A pair of brackets that can be used instead of a comma or dash. (see brackets.)

passive voice: The object is moved to the start of the sentence and is given a subject function.

Passive voice

Object	Verb	Subject
the action is being done to	the action	carries out the action

The mouse was chased by the cat.

Active voice

Subject	Verb	Object
carries out the action	the action	the action is being done to

The cat chased the mouse.

past tense: Past tense refers to events that have happened in the past. There are four forms of past tense.

Past simple

regular- verb + ed | **irregular**

I walked
you walked
he walked
she walked
it walked
you walked
we walked
they walked

I ate
you ate
he ate
she ate
it ate
you ate
we ate
they ate

Past continuous

(was, were) + verb + 'ing'

I was running
you were running
he was running
she was running
it was running
you were running
we were running
they were running

Past perfect

had + past verb

I had danced
you had danced
he had danced
she had danced
it had danced
you had danced
we had danced
they had danced

Past perfect continuous

had + been + verb +ing

I had been dancing
you had been dancing
he had been dancing
she had been dancing
it had been dancing
you had been dancing
we had been dancing
they had been dancing

A-Z English Dictionary

personal pronoun: A word that identifies who is speaking, writing or being spoken to.

singular	plural
I/me	you/you
you/you	we/us
he/him	they/them
she/her	

personification: Figurative language in which something non-human is given a human characteristic.

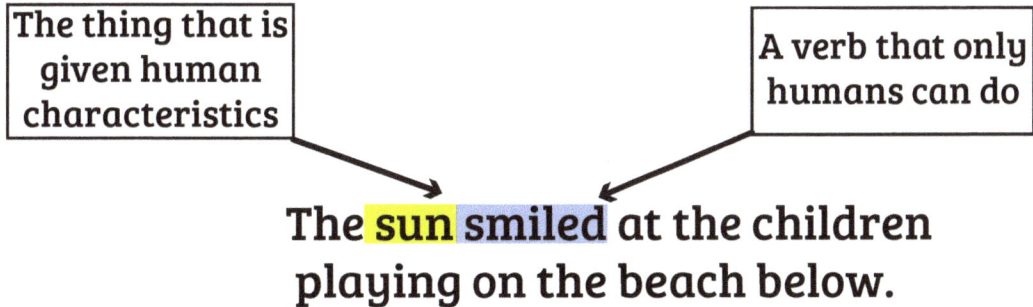

The sun smiled at the children playing on the beach below.

(The thing that is given human characteristics → sun; A verb that only humans can do → smiled)

persuasive text: A piece of writing from only one point of view. The purpose of the text is to persuade the reader to believe this same point of view.

phonics: A method of teaching people to read by learning specific letters or letter combinations and the sounds they make.

/c - a - t/ ⟶ cat

/ow/ ⟶ owl   cloud

phrase: A group of words that come together and form part of a clause. A phrase is not a sentence as it is not a complete idea and does not have a subject or verb. A phrase can function as:

    <u>Noun</u> - The yellow bird flew away.

    <u>Adjective</u> - He had piercing eyes.

    <u>Adverb</u> - She walked really slowly.

    <u>Prepositional</u> - After several minutes, I found the keys for the car.

picture books: A book where the illustrations (pictures) play a big part in telling the story.

plan: To develop and write your ideas when starting to write a text. Planning requires organising your ideas into sections and thinking about the purpose of the text and the audience who will read it.

play script: A piece of writing that is written to be performed. A play script includes a list of characters at the beginning and will also include stage directions that tell the actors where and when to move.

plural: A word that shows when there is more than one. It is usually signalled by adding 's'. However, some words are irregular or follow a specific spelling pattern.

Word endings	Rule	Examples
regular	add - s	1 book - 2 books 1 pencil - 2 pencils
irregular	no rule	1 tooth - 2 teeth 1 person - 2 people
ends in f or fe	remove f/fe add - ves	1 knife - 2 knives 1 wolf - 2 wolves
ends in s, ch, sh, x or z	add - es	1 box - 2 boxes 1 dish - 2 dishes
ends in vowel + y	add - s	1 toy - 2 toys 1 key - 2 keys
ends in consonant + y	remove y add - ies	1 baby - 2 babies 1 story - 2 stories
ends in vowel + o	add - s	1 radio - 2 radios 1 zoo - 2 zoos
ends in consonant + o	add - es	1 hero - 2 heroes 1 tomato - 2 tomatoes
no change	no change	1 sheep - 2 sheep 1 species - 2 species

poem: A type of writing that uses artistic styles such as rhyme, rhythm and figurative language to stir the imagination and emotions of the reader.

polysyllabic: A word that has many syllables.

Polysyllabic words

biography - bi - o - gra - phy
figurative - fig - ur - at - ive
chronological - chron - ol - og - ic - al

possessive pronoun: A pronoun that shows ownership.

Pronoun	Possessive Pronoun
I	my/mine
you	your/yours
he	his
she	her/hers
it	its
we	our/ours
they	their/theirs

A-Z English Dictionary

powerful verb: A verb that is chosen because it has precise meaning. Using powerful verbs can make a big difference to your writing.

I walked across the field.　　| walked is just walked no extra information |

I ambled across the field.　　| ambled means to move quite slowly |

prefix: A group of letters that can be added to the beginning of some words. Prefixes have their own meaning and can help give clues about the meaning of words they are added to.

Prefix	Meaning	Example
re	again	rewrite
un	not	unhappy
dis	opposite of	dissatisfied
pre	before	preview
tri	three	triangle
mis	wrong	misspelt
non	not	nonsense

preposition: A preposition is a word that shows the relationship between a noun or pronoun with something else in the sentence. It usually tells us the position of the noun.

prepositional phrase: Connects an object to the preposition.

I want to eat some food before we start the meeting.

Our hotel is near the ocean.

present tense: Present tense refers to events that are happening right now. There are four forms of present tense.

Present simple

I walk
you walk
he walks
she walks
it walks
you walk
we walk
they walk

Present continuous

(am, is, are) + verb + 'ing'

I am running
you are running
he is running
she is running
it is running
you are running
we are running
they are running

Present perfect

(have, has + past verb)

I have danced
you have danced
he has danced
she has danced
it has danced
you have danced
we have danced
they have danced

Present perfect continuous

(have, has) + been + verb +ing

I have been dancing
you have been dancing
he has been dancing
she has been dancing
it has been dancing
you have been dancing
we have been dancing
they have been dancing

presentation (i): How a piece of learning looks and how it appeals to the reader.

presentation (ii): To share and show a piece of learning to an audience. The presentation may be evaluated and assessed by other students and/or the teacher.

pronoun: A word class that is used to replace nouns. (See also personal, possessive and reflexive pronoun.)

A-Z English Dictionary

proofread: To check a piece of writing for errors and mistakes.

proverb: An old saying that has a lesson or message about life. Proverbs come from all over the world but the lessons are easy for everyone to understand.

Proverb	Origin	Meaning
Give a man a fish, he can eat for a day; teach a man how to fish, he can eat for a lifetime.	Asia	Teaching people is better than doing things for them.
Absence makes the heart grow fonder.	N. America	When you are apart from someone, you miss them and like them even more.
Since we cannot get what we like, let us like what we can get.	Spain	Appreciate and be thankful for what we have.

pun: A joke that uses a play on words. A pun usually can have two different meanings which makes it funny.

What do you mean I am not a bear! I have Koalafications.

punctuation: Punctuation is used to separate sentences and to help clarify meaning. Examples of punctuation include: full stop, comma, speech marks, brackets and colons.

Name	Mark	Name	Mark
full stop	.	brackets	()
comma	,	colon	:
question mark	?	semi colon	;
apostrophe	'	dash	—
exclamation mark	!	hyphen	-

purpose: The reason why an oral or written text is produced. The purpose is the 'why' it was made. For example, is the text to inform? Instruct? Persuade or entertain?

question mark: A punctuation mark that is placed at the end of a sentence when a question has been asked.

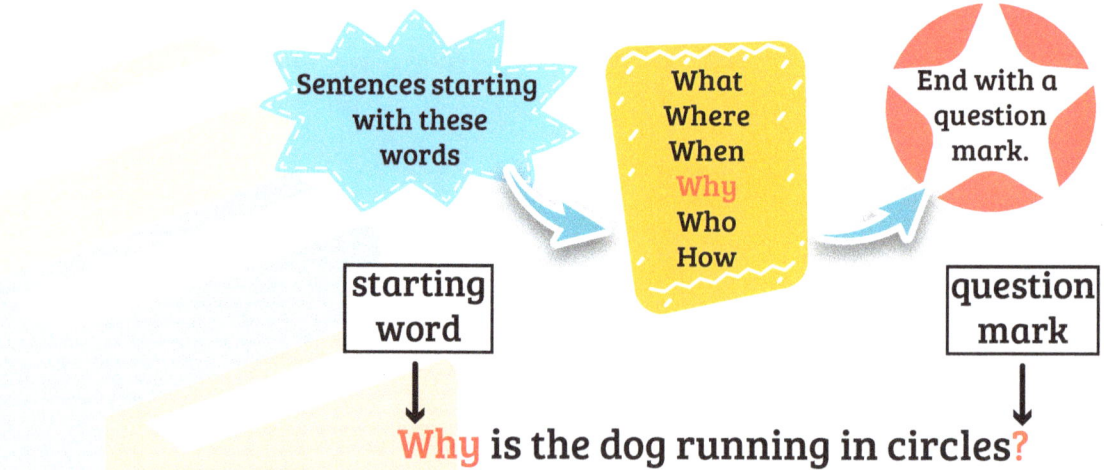

A-Z English Dictionary

questioning: A technique of asking a range of different questions about about a subject or issue. Questioning is a very good strategy when you want to find out as much information as possible.

rap: A form of rhyming poetry that is spoken. Rap is often accompanied with music or repetitive beat and can be spoken rhythmically and at pace.

reading aloud: Saying what you are reading so that it can help to improve expression and get a clearer understanding of punctuation.

reading scheme: A collection of reading books that increase in difficulty as you progress through the scheme.

recount: A genre of writing whose purpose is to retell and inform the audience about an event. It can be fictional with characters, dialogue and setting. It can also be non-fictional in the form of a diary, newspaper report or a biography.

reference: A type of book that is arranged alphabetically in order to help the reader retrieve information. e.g. dictionary, atlas, encyclopedia.

reflexive pronoun: A type of pronoun that ends in self or selves.

Pronoun	Reflexive Pronoun
I	myself
you	yourself
he	himself
she	herself
it	itself
you	yourselves
we	ourselves
they	themselves

regular verb: A verb that has standard patterns and rules.

rehearse: To practice a skill such as reading, singing, performing in readiness to perform in front of an audience.

A-Z English Dictionary

relative clause: A specific type of subordinate clause that begins with a relative pronoun. (See relative pronoun.)

Sasha liked her new jumper which was brightly coloured.
                                 ⎵⎵⎵⎵⎵⎵⎵⎵⎵⎵⎵⎵⎵⎵⎵⎵⎵⎵⎵⎵⎵⎵
                                         relative clause

Daniel, who plays baseball for the Tigers, scored a home run today.
        ⎵⎵⎵⎵⎵⎵⎵⎵⎵⎵⎵⎵⎵⎵⎵⎵⎵⎵⎵⎵⎵⎵⎵⎵⎵⎵⎵⎵
                    relative clause

relative pronoun: A type of pronoun that refers to the noun that has already been mentioned in the sentence.

relative pronoun	noun that the pronoun refers to
who	refers to a person
which	refers to an animal, place or thing
that	refers to an animal, place or thing

A-Z English Dictionary

report: A piece of writing that gives information about a particular subject. A non-chronological report is not written in time order and is usually written in the present tense.

resolution: In story writing, the resolution is the part where the main problem or conflict of the story has come to an end and has been resolved.

retell: To tell a story in your own words without looking at the original text.

rhetorical question: A type of question where the person who has asked the question does not expect an answer. Rhetorical questions can have no answer or the answer can be really obvious.

<u>obvious answer</u>

Is this supposed to be some kind of joke?

<u>no answer</u>

How many times do I have to ask?

A-Z English Dictionary

rhyme: When words have similar sounds either within the word or at the end of the word.

school - cool
teacher - creature

rhythm: The heavy and soft beats that appear in music and speech.

riddle: A type of poem that describes something without naming it. The reader has to try and guess what it is.

role play: Taking on the role of a character to understand what the character thinks and feels in a particular situation. Role play is a good way to develop a deeper understanding of the character you are reading about or the character you want to write about in your own story.

scaffolding: A strategy where the teacher provides support and/or resources to help the student understand a teaching point. The student will gradually understand, become more independent and occasionally use the supporting resources.

scan: To read a text very quickly to find and retrieve facts or pieces of information.

A-Z English Dictionary

science fiction: A genre of writing that deals with future advances in science or technology and often involves, space flight, other worlds or significant changes to this world because of new technology.

scribe: A person who writes down what is spoken.

scribing: The process of writing down what is being spoken.

semi colon: A punctuation mark (;) used to join two independent clauses that are closely related in meaning.

1. Used to replace a full stop between two main clauses that are closely linked.

   I was told I couldn't go swimming**;** I didn't want to go anyway.
   (semi colon)

2. Used to replace a coordinating conjunction of two closely related main clauses.

   Oranges are a healthy snack**;** they are full of vitamin C.
   (semi colon)

A-Z English Dictionary

sequel: A text or film that follows on from the original.

setting: The place or type of surroundings where a story takes place.

shape poem: (See concrete poem.)

simile: A form of figurative language where two things are compared to one another using the words 'like' or 'as'.

Example 1:

The carpet was as thick as a layer of freshly fallen snow.

- use *as* to compare
- two things are being compared

Example 2:

Grandad lounged on the raft in the middle of the pool like an old battleship.

- two things are being compared
- use *like* to compare

simple sentence: A sentence that contains one clause. It has to have a subject and a verb.

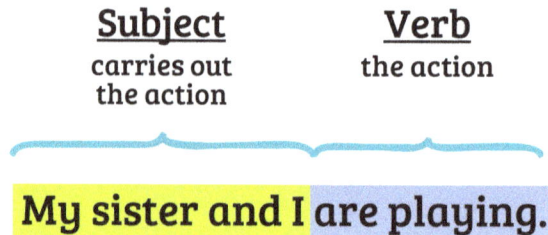

singular: A word that refers to just one thing.

singular

1 book - 2 books
1 pencil - 2 pencils

speech bubble: A way to show a character's speech. Often used in illustrations and comic books.

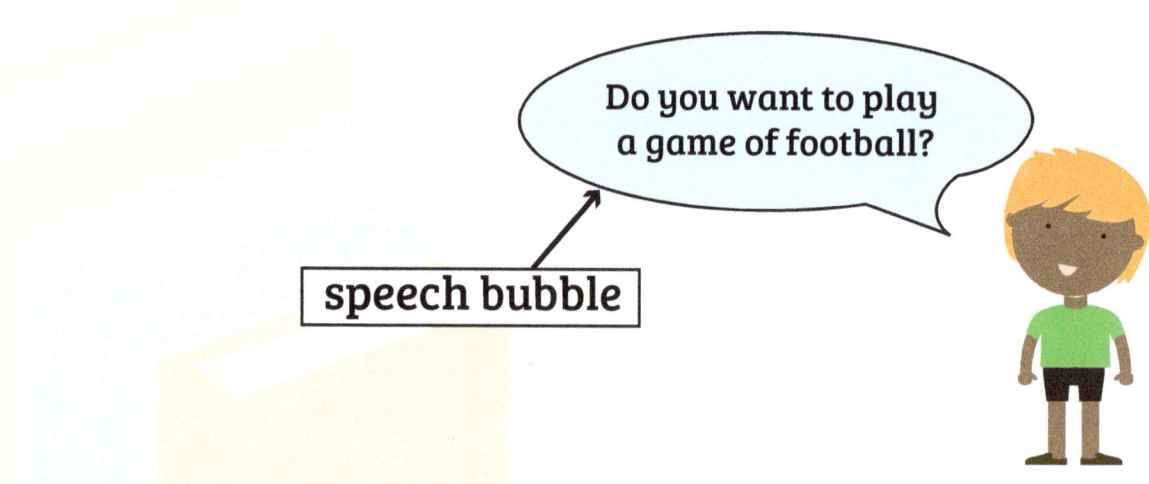

A-Z English Dictionary

speech marks: A punctuation mark (".."") that is used to show when a character is speaking.

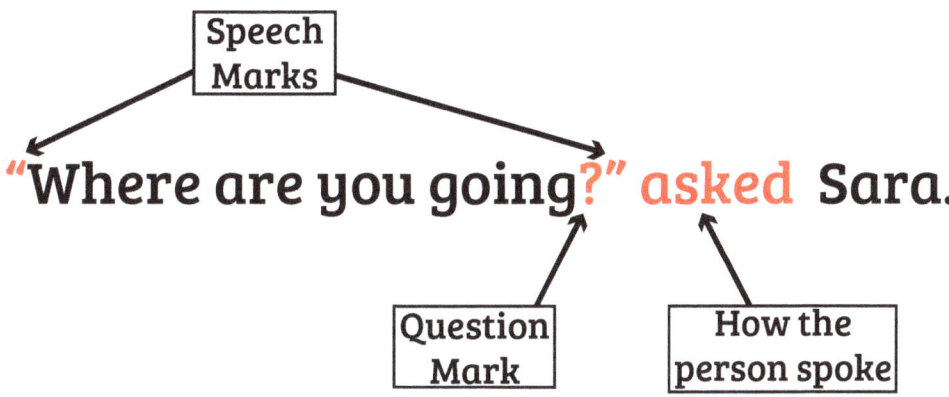

stanza: Another name for a verse in a poem.

statement: A sentence that gives the reader information and ends with a full stop.

Danny is going to buy a new car today. statement

story: Narrative fiction that is usually told in chronological order. A story will include, characters, setting and a problem that comes to a resolution towards the end.

A-Z English Dictionary

story structure: The way a story is put together. The structure of most stories includes: beginning, middle and an ending.

subheading: An organisational device used in non-fiction texts. A subheading or subtitle is used to help organise a text into smaller categories that are related to the main title.

TITLE

subheading

Text

subject: A person, place or thing that is being or doing the action of the sentence.

Subject	Verb	Object
carries out the action	the action	the action is being done to

The cat chased the mouse.

Subject	Verb
is being	being

The weather is cold today.

subordinate clause: Aso called a dependent clause. A clause that does not make sense on its own. For a subordinate clause to make sense it can be added before or after the main clause or alternatively be embedded within the main clause.

(i) subordinate clause before main clause

Although the boy was hungry, he didn't eat breakfast.

- Although the boy was hungry → Subordinate Clause
- he didn't eat breakfast → Main Clause

(ii) subordinate clause after the main clause

The boy didn't eat breakfast *although he was hungry.*

- The boy didn't eat breakfast → Main Clause
- although he was hungry → Subordinate Clause

(iii) subordinate clause embedded in the main clause.

The boy, *although he was hungry,* didn't eat any breakfast.

- The boy → Main Clause
- although he was hungry → Subordinate Clause
- didn't eat any breakfast → Main Clause

subordinate conjunction: A type of conjunction that is used in a subordinate clause.

although	if
because	where
after	when
as	unless
even though	until
before	while

suffix: A letter or group of letters that are added to the end of a word and can change either the grammatical function of the word or change the meaning.

suffix	meaning	example
-less	without	worthless
-ed	changes to past tense	looked
-ible	able to	edible

summarise: To write or talk about the main points of a text or speech.

superlative: An adjective that describes something to its highest degree.

one syllable add 'est'	two syllables words end in 'y' remove 'y' add 'iest'	two or more syllables add 'most'
big - bigg**est**	early - earl**iest**	beautiful - **most** beautiful
old - old**est**	easy - eas**iest**	intelligent - **most** intelligent
small - small**est**	happy - happ**iest**	difficult - **most** difficult

suspense: A technique in narrative writing where the writer delays revealing something so that the audience feels anticipation, nervousness or excitement as to what may happen next.

syllable: A single unbroken sound of a spoken or written word.

one syllable	two syllables	three syllables
chat - chat	water - wa / ter	chocolate - cho / co / late
light - light	freezing - free / zing	banana - ba / na / na

A-Z English Dictionary

synonym: A word that has a similar meaning to another word.

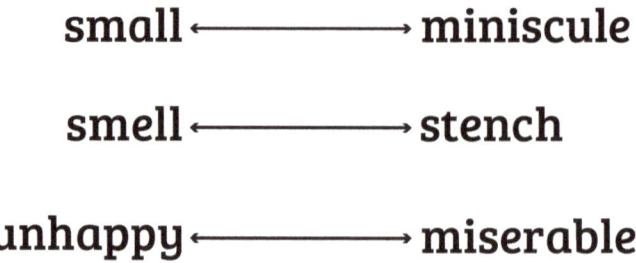

small ⟷ miniscule

smell ⟷ stench

unhappy ⟷ miserable

talk for writing: A strategy to help develop writing. Children may retell a story they know or tell a story of their own. Puppets, pictures and props can be used. The process is to help the student think about vocabulary, sentences and the structure of the story.

talk partner: A learning technique where the teacher will ask children to share their ideas and thinking with a partner.

teacher talk: A teaching teachnique where the teacher will talk out loud and share their thinking as they demonstrate how to complete an activity. Understanding what the teacher is thinking can help the student develop their own thinking skills.

A-Z English Dictionary

tense: The way a verb shows you when something happened is called tense. The three main tenses are: past, present and future.

text: A piece of writing that follows the criteria of a genre, e.g. poetry, fantasy, instructions.

text type: (See genre.)

thesaurus: A reference book that that has words in alphebetical order. Instead of explaining the meaning of each word, a thesaurus lists words that have the same or similar meanings.

tongue twister: A sentence that is worded using alliteration so that it is very difficult to say when spoken quickly.

I see seashells on the sea floor.

Peter Piper picked a peck of pickled pepper.

topic sentence: The first sentence of a paragraph that introduces and summarises what the paragraph is about.

topic - The International Space Station

topic sentence - The International Space Station is an orbiting space craft where astronauts can conduct experiments.

traditional tale: A short story that is written or spoken and passed through generations of a particular culture.

Japanese - Momotaro

European - Goldilocks and the Three Bears

trilogy: A series of three books that contain the same characters and setting.

underline: To draw a line under a word, phrase or sentence so that it will stand out in the text.

This sentence is underlined.

upper case: Letters of the alphabet which are capital letters.

Aa Bb Cc Dd Ee Ff Gg Hh Ii Jj Kk Ll Mm

Nn Oo Pp Qq Rr Ss Tt Uu Vv Ww Xx Yy Zz

A-Z English Dictionary

verb: One of the main word classes. Verbs can be actions, states of being e.g. I am, a thought or a feeling.

verb phrase: A verb phrase consists of an auxilary verb, or helping verb and the main verb.

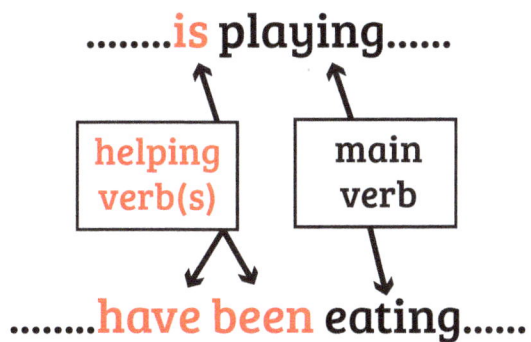

viewpoint (i): The position of the viewer when they are looking at a picture or scenery.

viewpoint (ii): A person's opinion or point of view on a subject or topic.

viewpoint (iii): The point of view of a character from a story.

visual cue: A picture or visual image readers use to help them understand and interpret a text.

visualisation: A teaching strategy where children are asked to close their eyes and imagine the details of a scene or situation. The teacher often guides the children by talking them through it. This can be useful to help children create their own ideas.

vocabulary: Individual words used in a particular language.

voice (i): The difference between <u>active</u> and <u>passive</u>.

voice (ii): The perspective of the character in a story.

A-Z English Dictionary

vowel: Letters in the alphabet a , e , i , o , u.

vowels	consonants
Aa Ee Ii Oo Uu	Bb Cc Dd Ff Gg Hh Jj Kk Ll Mm Nn Pp Qq Rr Ss Tt Vv Ww Xx Yy Zz

word class: Words that have a particular function in a sentence. The main word classes are: verb, adjective, noun, pronoun, adverb, preposition, determiner and conjunction.

She walked carefully on the icy pavement because it was slippery.

- Pronoun: replaces a noun
- Verb: action or being word
- Adverb: describes the verb
- Preposition: explains position

- Determiner: identifies the noun
- Noun: thing or person
- Conjunction: joins ideas
- Adjective: describing word

writing frame: A writing resource that is used during the planning stage of writing. A writing frame often includes structural features of the text which supports the child in organising the text.

writing in role: Taking on the perspective of a character and writing from their point of view. Writing in role is very helpful after doing drama activities such as hot seating.

www.ingramcontent.com/pod-product-compliance
Lightning Source LLC
Chambersburg PA
CBHW042015090526
44587CB00027B/4268